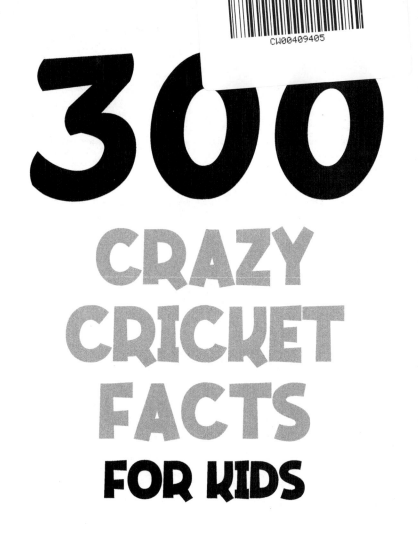

300

CRAZY CRICKET FACTS

FOR KIDS

ALL FACTS ARE
CORRECT AS OF
DECEMBER 2021

CW00409405

Cricket bats are made from a wood called white willow.

The first Cricket World Cup was played in England in 1975.

A cricket ball must weigh exactly 163g (5.75 ounces)

The three sticks a bowler is trying to knock over are called the stumps.

Oliver Cromwell is reported to have played cricket in London

The highest number of runs scored by a batter in an over is 36 by Herschelle Gibbs of South Africa.

Famous England cricketer Kevin Pietersen was actually born in South Africa

---

The first cricket ball was made of wool

The two small pieces of wood, balanced on top of the stumps are called the bails.

The longest cricket match on record was 14 days long!

The end of a day's play in a test match is called 'stumps'.

A bowler can only bowl 6 bowls consecutively which is an 'over'

A cricket pitch is also called a wicket.

When cricket first started there were only two stumps, not three.

A century is when a batter scores 100 runs without getting out.

---

111 is said to be an unlucky score in cricket.

The catchers that stand next to the wicket keeper are called the slips.

A cricket pitch is exactly 22 yards long.

A batter can score a run by hitting the ball and then running to the other end of the wicket.

The rope around the edge of the pitch is called the boundary.

If the batter hits the ball and it crosses the boundary rope, hitting the floor beforehand, the batter scores 4 runs.

A batter can also score a run by hitting the ball over the boundary rope.

If the batter hits the ball over the boundary rope without the ball touching the ground first, they score 6 runs.

If the batter hits the ball with their bat or glove and the other team catches the ball, the batter is out.

A cricket match is played between 2 teams of 11 players.

Ball marks left on cricket bats are called 'cherries'

There are 4 different types of cricket match: The 100, T20, One day and Test Match.

If a player allows the ball to hit their pads in front of the stumps, they are out - lbw (leg before wicket)

In a 100 match, each team has 100 balls to score runs or get the other team out.

In a T20 match, each side has twenty overs (120 balls) to score runs and get the other team out.

In a One Day match, each team has 50 overs to score runs and get the other team out.

In a test match, both teams bat and bowl twice and it can take up to 5 days to complete a match.

Test matches can still end in a draw, even after 5 days of play.

A cricket pitch or wicket is 3 metres wide.

If a batsman is out for no runs, it is called a 'duck'.

An easy catch is often called a 'lolly', a 'dolly' or a 'sitter'.

A ball where no run is scored is called a 'dot ball'.

The 'circle' or 'fielding circle' is a line marked out 30m in radius around the wicket.

When the batting team don't score any runs in an over, it is a called a maiden over.

The record number of maidens bowled consecutively is 21 by Indian spin bowler Bapu Nadkarni in 1954 vs England.

Cricket is played in 92 countries.

The 'nervous nineties' are when a batsman has scored between 91 and 99 and they are getting nervous about scoring a century.

If the ball hits the edge of the bat and it is caught by a fielder, it is called an 'edge'. It is also referred to as a 'nick' or a 'tickle'.

DRS (Decision Review System) was first introduced in 2008.

The first batter to be given out using DRS was Virender Sehwag.

When a decision is reviewed, the third umpire uses a range of technology to check the decision. They check for a no-ball, check if the ball has been edged, check if the ball has pitched in the line of the stumps, and if the ball was going to hit the stumps.

To check if the ball has touched the bat, an infrared camera is used. This is called 'hot spot'.

If a team successfully reviews a decision, they keep the referral. Each team has 2 referrals per innings so they must use them wisely.

The line in front of the stumps where the batter prepares to face the ball is called the crease.

The umpire has a series or signals to signify what happened for the crowd and the scorers.

England have been all out for less than 100 runs in an Ashes test 21 times.

There have been 72 Ashes series: Australia have won 34 and England have won 32. There have been 6 draws.

In the Ashes, Australia have recorded 3 whitewashes, winning every test. England have never recorded a whitewash.

The smallest margin of victory in an Ashes test was achieved by England, in 2005, winning by 2 runs.

The lowest total recorded in the Ashes was the 36 runs Australia scored in 1902.

The highest total ever recorded in an Ashes test was the 903/7 by England in 1938.

The highest score in an Ashes test by a batsman was the 364 recorded by England player Len Hutton in 1938.

Australian spinner, Shane Warne holds the record for most total wickets taken in the Ashes at 172 wickets from 31 matches.

Every cricket ground has two sight screens. These are large white screens at either end of the ground, that are moved into position, so the batsman can see the ball being released from the hand of the bowler.

Eden Gardens, in Kolkata, India, is the oldest cricket ground in India, built in 1864. It is known as the Mecca of Indian cricket.

The most controversial Ashes series was the Bodyline Tour of 1932-3 when England targeted the bodies and heads of the Australian batters with their bowling. Many Australian players retired hurt, struck by England's aggressive bowling.

Melbourne cricket ground in Australia, was built in 1853 and it is one of the biggest ground in the world, holding over 100,000 spectators.

The recently built Narendra Modi stadium in Motera, Ahmedabad is the largest cricket venue in the world, seating 132,000 spectators.

The WACA cricket ground, in Perth, Australia, is known for having the fastest pitch in the world.

When a team thinks they have got a batter out they shout 'Howzat' and look at the umpire. They are asking the umpire 'How's that?' or is the player out? The umpire then decides if the batsman is out or not.

When the umpire lifts up their knee and touches it, this means the runs scored came off the leg and not the bat. These are called leg byes.

When the umpire extends his right arm straight up, it means the runs came off another part of the body. These are called byes.

When it is beginning to get dark, the umpires use a light meter and they 'offer the light' to the batting team, who can choose to suspend the play until it gets lighter or end the day if it is in the evening.

It is the umpire's job to count the 6 balls in the over. When it is complete, he calls 'over'.

When the umpire extends his right arm straight out to the side, it means it is a 'no ball'.

A 'no ball' is called when the bowler oversteps the crease when he is bowling the ball.

When a bowler bowls a no ball, they have to bowl another ball.

When the umpire makes a sweeping motion with his right arm, the batter has scored four runs.

The batting team are organised into a set order for batting. This is called the 'batting order'.

The first two batsman in a new innings are called the 'opening batsman' or 'openers'.

The last few batsman in a team are non-specialist batsman, usually the bowlers and they are often referred to as 'lower order batsmen', the 'tail' or 'tail enders'.

If the lower order batsmen score a few runs it is often said that 'the tail is wagging'.

When the umpire raises both arms and points at the sky, the batter has scored a six.

In a test match, the new ball is offered to the bowling team after 80 overs.

When the umpire extends both arms out sideways, it means the bowler bowled too wide. When a bowler bowls a wide, the batting team get an extra run added to their total and the ball has to be bowled again.

A cricket ball can be red, white or pink.

To signal that the new ball has been taken, the umpire holds it up in the air in his right hand.

The Marylebone Cricket Club were the first cricket team, formed in 1793.

The Marylebone Cricket Club were the first cricket team, formed in 1793.

A cricket bat is about 3ft (1m) in length.

The Marylebone Cricket Club (MCC) play their matches at Lords Cricket Ground, the 'home' of cricket.

International cricket matches have been played since 1844.

The first cricket bats were bent like hockey sticks.

The laws of cricket changed in 1877 which stated that the bats had to be straight.

A cricket bat is flat on the front and υ shaped on the back.

The bottom of the bat is called the toe.

The maximum width for a cricket bat is 4.25 inches (108mm).

The handle of a cricket bat is wrapped in rubber for better grip.

Linseed oil is rubbed into the bat to make it stronger.

In 1979, the cricket laws were changed to make it a rule that all bats had to be made of wood.

Denis Lillee had a cricket bat the was made partly of aluminium, called the 'combat bat'.

The process of making a bat is called 'podshaving'.

A cricket bat has two parts, the handle and the blade.

Cricket was originally a game for children.

The captain of the bowling team tells his team where to stand when they are fielding.

The stumps are 28 inches (71cm) high and 9 inches (22.86cm) wide in total.

The crease that the bowler must not step over is called the 'popping crease'.

The batters have to run a distance of 58ft (17.68m) from wicket to wicket.

The player who stands behind the stumps wearing gloves is called the wicket keeper.

There are over 30 different fielding positions and some of them have really unusual names, like silly mid off.

The sides of the pitch are called the on side or the off side, depending on whether the batter is right handed or left handed.

If the batter is right handed, the field to the left is the onside.

If the batter is right handed, the field to the right is the offside.

Every cricket match starts with a coin toss to decide who will bat first or who will bowl first, with the winner getting to choose.

A line of players in the slips is called the slips cordon.

There are two main types of bowler: a pace bowler or a spin bowler.

A pace bowler or fast bowler can bowl at 150km/h (93mph) or more.

A spin bowler uses the hand and wrist to spin the ball.

A fast bowler can bowl the ball short and hard into the pitch making the ball bounce towards the batter's head. This is called a bouncer or bumper.

With the right conditions, a fast bowler can sometimes swing the ball into or away from the batter.

Sometimes a fast bowler will bowl a slower ball to confuse the batter.

A cricket ball has a raised edge running around the ball, where the two halves of the ball are stitched together. This is called the seam.

A fast bowler can use bowl so the seam hits the pitch, causing the ball to deviate or bounce more.

A fast bowler can bowl a ball directly at the batsman's feet in front of the stumps – this is called a yorker.

If the batter hits the ball before the ball has bounced it is called a full toss.

The score in cricket is presented as the number of runs scored and the number of batters out. E.g. 55/3 is 55 runs with 3 batters out.

Batters first started wearing cricket pads in the mid 1700s.

There are four main types of spin bowler: Right arm leg break, right arm off break, left arm Chinaman, left arm orthodox.

There are many different techniques to spinning the ball, either spinning the ball towards the batter, away from the batter, or straight on.

Cricket pads were originally fastened using leather straps.

Spin bowling has some unusual names for the type of ball bowled, such as 'googly' or the 'wrong-un'.

Both batters and the wicket keeper from the bowling side wear pads to protect them from the ball.

Cricket pads come in all shapes and sizes, protecting the ankles, shins, knees and lower thighs.

When cricket pads first became popular, batters just let the ball bounce off their pads.

Modern cricket pads are fastened using three Velcro straps.

The laws of cricket changed in 1774 to stop players using their cricket pads to deflect the ball – Leg Before Wicket was introduced.

Wicket keepers used to use the same pads as batters, but in the modern game, wicket keeper pads a smaller.

Some batters use thigh pads as well as cricket pads to protect their legs.

Batters protect their privates using a 'box' made from hard plastic in case they get hit in between the legs.

Batters wear cricket gloves to protect their hands from the ball.

Cricket gloves are traditionally made of leather.

Due to the fact that the ball can be travelling at nearly 100 mph, some batters also use arm guards and a chest guard.

A batter's gloves are considered part of the bat so if the ball touches their gloves and is caught, the batsman is out.

Cricket gloves are heavily padded. Even so, a direct hit by a cricket ball can still break the batsman's finger!

The first recorded use of padded headgear by a batsman was in the 1930s by English cricketer, Patsy Hendren.

The first protective helmet worn by a batsman was in 1977 by Dennis Amis, an Englishman.

It is not a law in cricket to wear a helmet when batting, although all cricketers do.

The last batsman who chose to not wear a helmet was Viv Richards of the West Indies, who retired in 1991.

In England, all batters, wicket keepers and fielders within 8m of the wicket must wear a helmet.

A cricket helmet is typically made from plastic, carbon fibre or fibreglass.

In New Zealand and India the batsman does not have to wear a helmet by law.

The helmet is often fitted with a metal face grill that prevents the ball from striking the face of the batter.

In international one day or T20 matches, teams wear the uniform of their country.

Every team has a Twelfth Man who is a substitute fielder in case a player needs to go off for treatment to an injury or retire hurt.

The T20 or one day uniforms are also called pyjamas.

In test match cricket, the teams wear cricket whites.

Since 2000, all international teams playing one day matches have worn coloured uniforms.

Cricket whites (also called flannels) are made up of trousers, a shirt and a sweater (often sleeveless).

Cricket whites are white or cream in colour.

In test matches, teams wear a hat or a cap with their national flag or emblem on it.

Cricket hats can be caps, wide brimmed sun hats to keep the sun out of the player's eyes, or floppy hats.

When a player is making their debut (their first appearance for their country) they are presented with a cap before the match starts.

The Australian cap is called the Baggy Green.

In T20 and One Day matches, each team bats for one 50 over innings and bowls for one 50 over innings.

Each fixed period of time that a team bats is called an innings.

In a test match, each team has two innings to bat and two innings to bowl.

There are two on field umpires in every game of cricket.

There is one off field umpire in every game of cricket called the third umpire.

A match can be suspended because of rain or bad light.

The umpires decide if a match is suspended.

When a batsman scores 100 runs, it is called a century.

When a batsman scores 50 runs, it is called a half-century.

A cricket games was once stopped because a pig ran onto the field.

The first recorded cricket game was played in 1646.

Former England captain Alec Stewart scored 8463 runs in his career. His birthday was 8/4/63!

The first century in a test match was scored by Charlie Bannerman of Australia in 1877.

Cricket was a sport played in the 1896 and 1900 Olympics.

The first international cricket match took place in 1844, between USA and Canada.

Jim Laker, an English cricketer, has the record for most wickets in a test match with 19.

There are 10 ways a batsman can get out in cricket.

Shoaib Ahktar is credited with bowling the fastest ball – it was 100.23 mph.

Brian Lara is the only player to score 400 runs in a test match innings.

South Africa's A B de Villiers has the record for scoring 100 off the fewest balls in a One Day International – 31 balls!

The first Cricket World Cup was in 1975.

South Africa's David Miller has the record for scoring 100 off the fewest balls in a T20 match – 35 balls!

New Zealand's Brendan McCullum has the record for the fastest test match 100 – 54 balls!

Mudassar Nazar from Pakistan has the record for the slowest 100 in an international test match – it took him 557 minutes. That's 9 hours and 17 minutes of batting!

The distance between the bowling crease and the popping crease is 4 ft.

The first Cricket World Cup was won by the West Indies.

The first televised test match in England was in 1938.

When a bowler bowls out 3 batters in consecutive balls it is called a 'hat-trick'.

Adam Gilchrist, former Australian wicket keeper played 96 consecutive tests after making his debut.

Hasan Raza from Pakistan is the youngest player to play a test match at 14 years and 277 days.

The youngest English player to play a test match was Brian Close, who made his debut in 1949 at the age of 18 years and 149 days.

Cricket is the second most popular world sport, after football.

William Gilbert (W.G.) Grace is considered as the father of cricket. He played amateur cricket in England and helped develop the sport.

---

31 countries in the world play international cricket but only 12 countries have qualified for test status.

The oldest cricket world championship is the ICC Women's Cricket World Cup which was first held in 1973.

The country with the most losses in international cricket is England.

England have played nearly 2000 international cricket matches, more than any other country.

The condition of the cricket pitch (wicket) may change the strategy of the team.

The core of a cricket ball is made of cork.

Women have been playing cricket since the 1700s.

Despite inventing cricket, England have only ever won one World Cup. The beat New Zealand in a super over in the final of the 2019 T20 World Cup.

Before the introduction of overarm bowling in the 1790s, bowlers used to bowl underarm.

India and Pakistan are considered the biggest rivals in cricket.

Muttiah Murilatharan, from Sri Lanka, holds the record for the most test wickets (800) and the most ODI wickets (534).

The oldest cricketer to play an international match is England's Wilfred Rhodes, who was 52.

111 is considered an unlucky score in cricket – it is called a 'nelson'. It is considered unlucky because it looks like 3 wickets with the bails knocked off.

In Australia, 87 is considered an unlucky score. It is called the 'devil's number' because 100 – 87 is 13.

England was the first country to play 1000 test matches. They passed this milestone in 2018.

The highest paid cricketer is Indian captain, Virat Kohli.

Ex Indian captain Sachin Tendulkar's nickname was the 'God of Cricket' because he is considered as one of the greatest batsman of all time.

Australia's Don Bradman is widely considered the greatest batsman of all time. He averaged 99.94 runs every time he went out to bat in a test match.

Don Bradman still holds 8 records in cricket, even though he retired in 1949.

He shares the record for most triple centuries scored (2) with Brian Lara from the West Indies.

He's also the only player to score more than 5000 runs against England.

He also holds the record for the most number of runs scored in a single day (309).

The most successful cricket captain in test matches is Ricky Ponting from Australia. While he was captain, Australia won 220 times.

The worst test batsman of all time is New Zealand's Chris Martin. He only ever achieved a score of more than 9 once in his career.

The oldest preserved cricket bat was made in 1729 and is kept at the Oval Cricket Ground, in London.

India's Virender Sehwag holds the record for the fastest triple century, taking only 278 balls to do so.

India's Rahul Dravid's nickname was 'The Wall' because of his amazing defence.

Chris Gayle, from the West Indies, holds the record for the fastest century scored in any form of cricket. It took him 30 balls!

India's Rahul Dravid is the only cricketer to score 100 in four consecutive test match innings.

Ex-Australian fast bowler, Glen McGrath is the only player to take a wicket on the last ball he bowled before retiring from T20, ODI and Test Match cricket.

The Ashes is a 5 test series played between England and Australia.

Even though test series between England and Australia had been happening since 1882, the series wasn't known as the Ashes series until the 1930s.

In the Ashes, both sides are competing to win a tiny urn, standing only 10.5cm tall and said to contain the ashes of a cricket bail.

The winning team of the Ashes is presented with a crystal urn replica of the original urn.

The real Ashes urn, which was originally presented to England captain Ivo Bligh when England regained the Ashes in Australia in 1883, is in the MCC Museum at Lord's cricket ground.

To win the 5 match Ashes series, the team that lost last time has to win the series outright. If the series is a draw, the Ashes stays with the previous winners.

Lord's cricket ground, in London is known as the home of cricket.

Lord's cricket ground has been the venue for 4 World Cup Finals.

Lord's was founded by Thomas Lord, a professional bowler who played from 1787 to 1802.

Lord's cricket ground houses the oldest sporting museum in the world.

The pitch at Lord's cricket ground has a slope of over two metres, helping bowlers and making it more tricky for the batsmen.

India has the most test match stadiums in the world with 28.

Eden Gardens in New Zealand is the smallest international cricket stadium in the world, with a straight on boundary of 55m and a square boundary of 65m.

The smallest international stadium in the world by capacity is The Grange Club stadium in Scotland which is the home of Scottish cricket and holds 5000 spectators.

Jason Gillespie, an Australian bowler, is the only nightwatchman ever to score a double century – and it was his last match!

New Zealand's Geoff Allot scored a duck after facing 77 balls without scoring.

The most extras (byes, leg byes and no balls) given in a test match was 76, by Pakistan, against India, in 2007.

The most balls bowled in an over is 17 by Mohammed Sami against Sri Lanka in the 2004 Asia Cup. He bowled 7 wides, 4 no-balls and leaked 15 runs.

When a batting team loses a lot of wickets for very few runs it is called a 'collapse'.

The record for the most runs scored by the last man batting is held by Ashton Agar of Australia who scored 98 in an Ashes test in 2013.

At the end of T20 or a ODI match, if the scores are level, there is a super over where each team bowls one more over. Whoever scores the most runs, wins.

A batter's footwork is their ability to use their feet to get into position to play a shot.

A batsman's strike rate is a percentage equal to the number of runs scored divided by the number of balls faced. If a player faces 50 balls and scores 25 runs, the strike rate is 50.

A batsman's average is the total number of runs scored divided by the number of times they were given out. If a player scored 5000 runs and got out 200 times, the batting average would be 25.

A bowler's strike rate is the average number of balls they need to bowl before taking a wicket. The number of balls bowled is divided by the number of wickets taken. If a player bowls 2000 balls and takes 50 wickets, they have a strike rate of 40.

Shahid Afridi, of Pakistan, has the best strike rate for test matches. He played 27 tests and had a strike rate of 86.97.

In test matches, the bowler with the best strike rate is George Lohmann, and English bowler who played from 1865 to 1901. His strike rate was 34.1.

A bowler's bowling average is calculated by the number of runs conceded by the number of wickets taken.

In test matches, English bowler George Lohmann also holds this record with an amazing average of 10.75.

The 'block hole' is the gap between the bottom of a player's bat and the ground. Bowlers use the yorker to try and get the ball through the 'block hole'.

A bowler who is good at not giving away runs and taking wickets at the end of a limited overs match is called a 'death bowler'.

The 'death rattle' is the clattering sound of the wickets being hit and the bails coming off.

In a test match, if a team scores a lot of runs without being bowled out, they can 'declare'. They have set a high target for the other team and they want to focus on bowling them out. Teams do this so the match can end in a positive result before the 5 days are up.

If a player is fielding near the boundary they are fielding in the 'deep'. They are also referred to as 'boundary riders'.

If a bowler knocks over the stumps without the batter hitting the ball, it is called 'clean bowled'.

If a batter hits the ball but it goes on to hit the stumps, they have 'played on' or 'chopped on'.

A 'direct hit' is when a fielder picks up the ball after it has been hit and throws it at the stumps, removing the bails before the batter has got in. The batter has been run out by a direct hit.

The Duckworth Lewis Method is a formula used to revise the scoring target for a batting team in a limited overs match that has been shortened because of rain.

A 'Golden Duck' is when a batter is dismissed for no runs from the first ball that they face.

A 'Golden Pair' or 'King Pair' is when a batter is out for no runs from the first ball they face two innings in a row.

If a batting team sets a high score and the opposing team are bowled out for much fewer runs, the team with the higher score may force the other team to 'follow on' which means they have to bat again. In a five day match the team need to get within 200 runs, in a 3 or 4 day match it is 150 runs.

There are three types of length that a bowler can bowl: short, good, and full.

If a batter plays a shot in the air, aiming for a four or a six and they are caught near the boundary, that are said to have 'holed out'.

A right arm bowler bowls 'over the wicket' when they pass the stumps to the left of the non-striker. A left arm bowler bowls 'over the wicket' when they pass to the right.

If two batters stay in and start scoring runs, it is called a 'partnership'.

A left arm bowler bowls 'around the wicket' when they pass the stumps to the left of the non-striker. A right arm bowler bowls 'around the wicket' when they pass to the right.

A bowler may choose to bowl from over or around the wicket to vary the angle of their delivery into the batsman.

In One Day Internationals, a bowler can bowl a maximum of 10 overs.

A powerplay is a period of time in a limited overs games where there are field restrictions to help the batting side.

In One Day Internationals, the powerplay happens in the first 10 overs when only 2 fielders are allowed outside of the circle.

In T20 matches, the powerplay is the first 6 overs when only 2 fielders are allowed outside of the circle.

In T20 matches, a bowler can bowl a maximum of 4 overs.

A team's run rate is the average number of runs they are scoring per over.

'Sledging' is when teams try to wind each other up verbally during a match.

If a batter is bowled by a ball that passes between bat and pad an then hist the stumps, they have been bowled 'through the gate'.

In a match between South Africa and Sri Lanka in the Cricket World Cup in 2019, play was suspended because a swarm of bees cam onto the pitch.

A 'Wicket Maiden' is when a bowler bowls a batsman out without giving away any runs in a single over.

In one of England's tour matches in India in 2012, play had to be suspended because some grey langur monkeys invaded the pitch.

In a South African league match in 1995, a six was hit out of the ground and it landed in a barbecue. It took a while to retrieve the ball and they had to wait for it to cool down before resuming play.

During a County Championship match at Lord's in 1980, a Canada goose landed on the pitch and started chasing the players.

In a One Day match between Australia and England in 1983, a fan let a piglet onto the pitch with the names of two England players written on either side. It took a while for the police to catch the piglet before play could resume.

The longest distance a cricket ball has ever been hit is 556 miles. In South Africa a player hit a ball out of the stadium and it landed on a passing train, travelling all the way to Port Elizabeth.

Play was suspended in a match at the Ageas Bowl in 2011 because of a sighting of white tiger nearby. The spectators and the players took cover, only for the authorities to discover that the tiger was only a stuffed toy.

Cricket umpires wear white coats so it's easier for the bastman to see the ball when the bowler releases it.

Mark Boucher, South African wicketkeeper, holds the record for the overall number of dismissals by a wicketkeeper across all forms of the game. He caught and stumped 999 wickets in his time, and bowled out one West Indian player, bringing his total to 1000.

India hold the record for being the first team to be bowled out twice in the same day. Zimbabwe have done it twice since.

Printed in Great Britain
by Amazon

83612578R00052